In his own light

Anthony D

When scribble was young he used to sit drawing with an anglepoise lamp.His mother used to say to him, 'You are sitting in your own light.' These are some of his recent charcoal drawings, he is an old man now.

Fig 1:Girl sitting scrunched up.

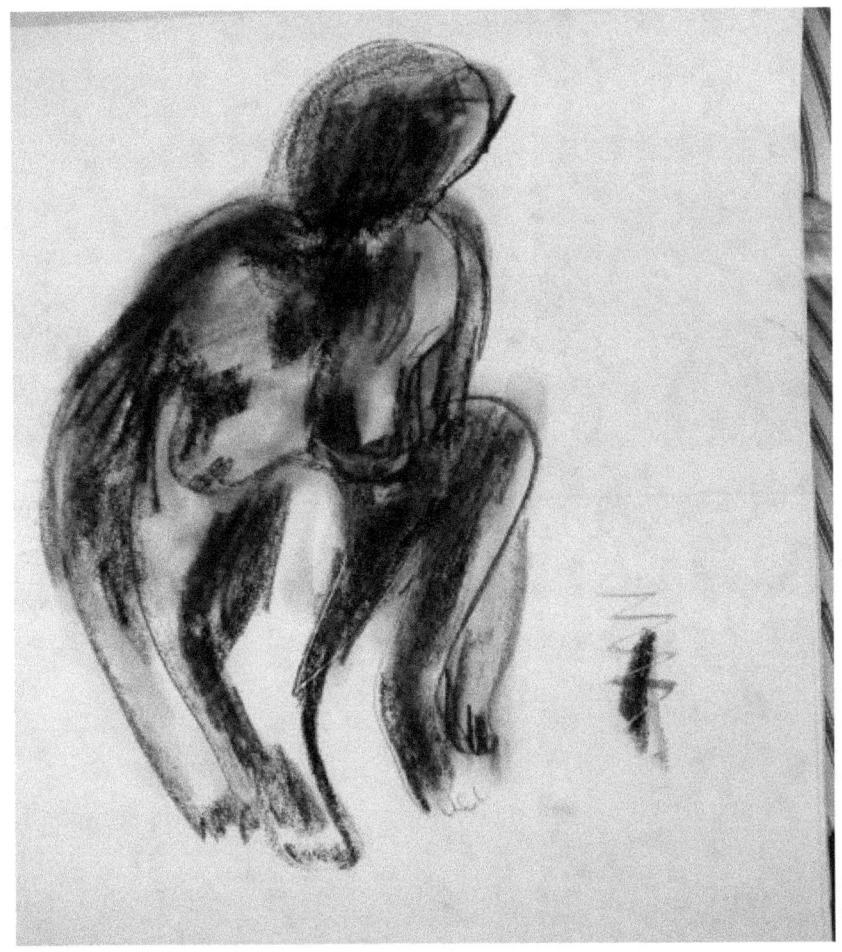

Fig 2:Girl kneeling

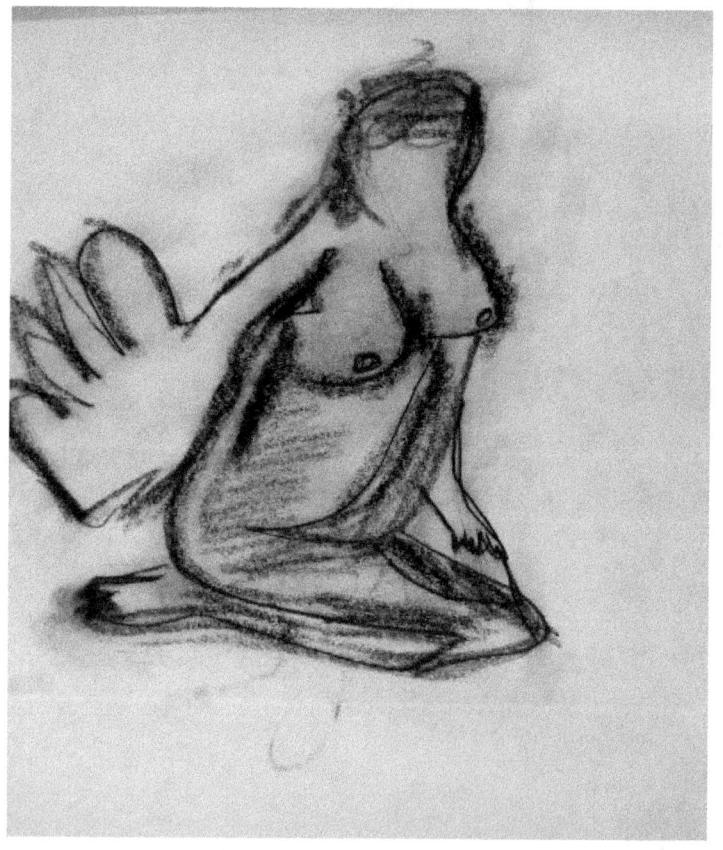

Fig 3: Woman on side

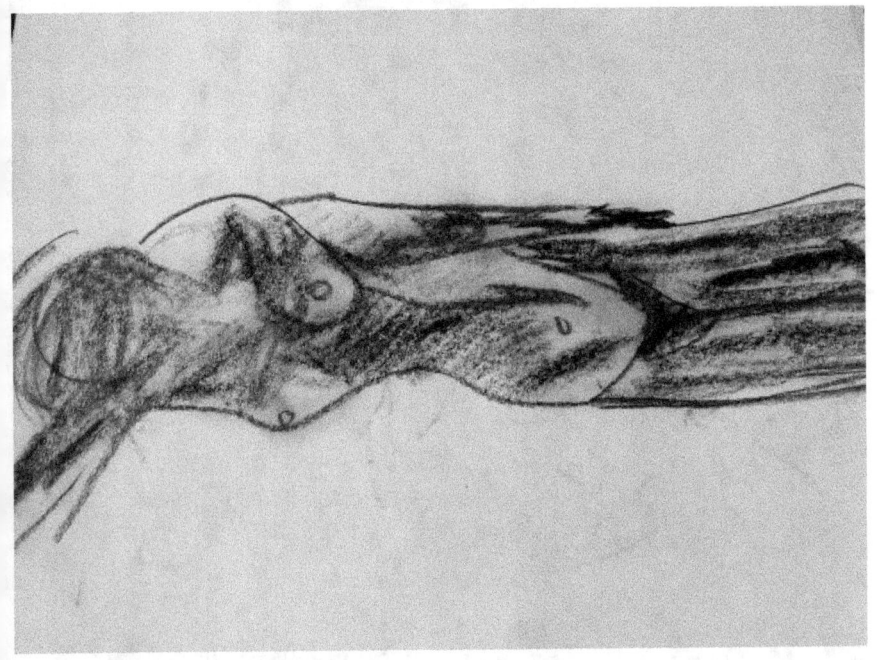

Fig 4:Woman sitting

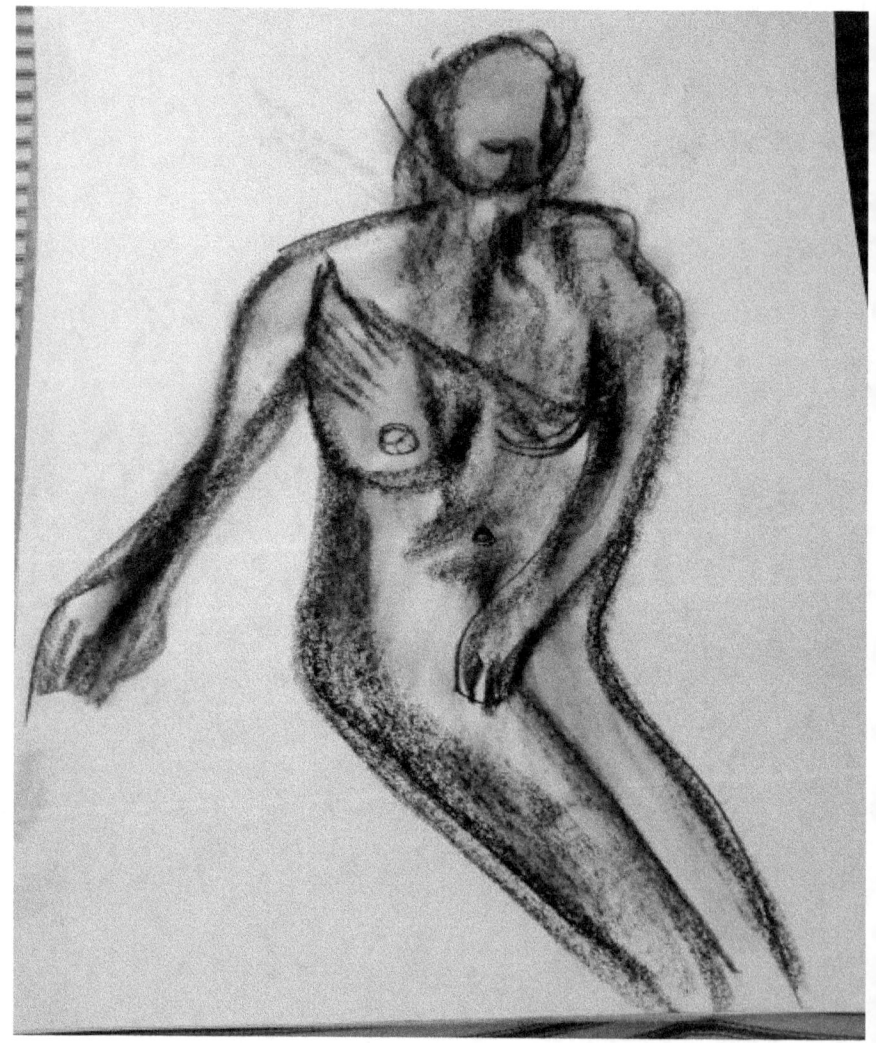

Fig 5:Old man sitting

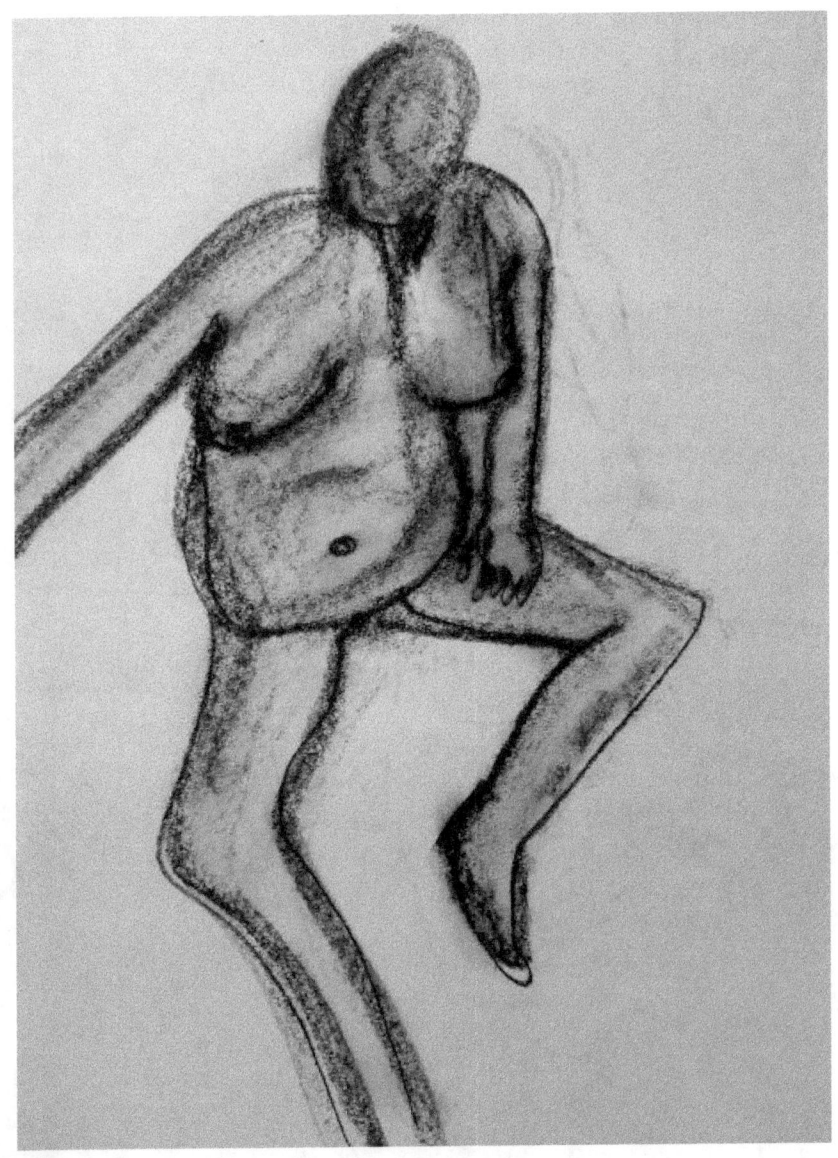

Fig 6:Breast of woman

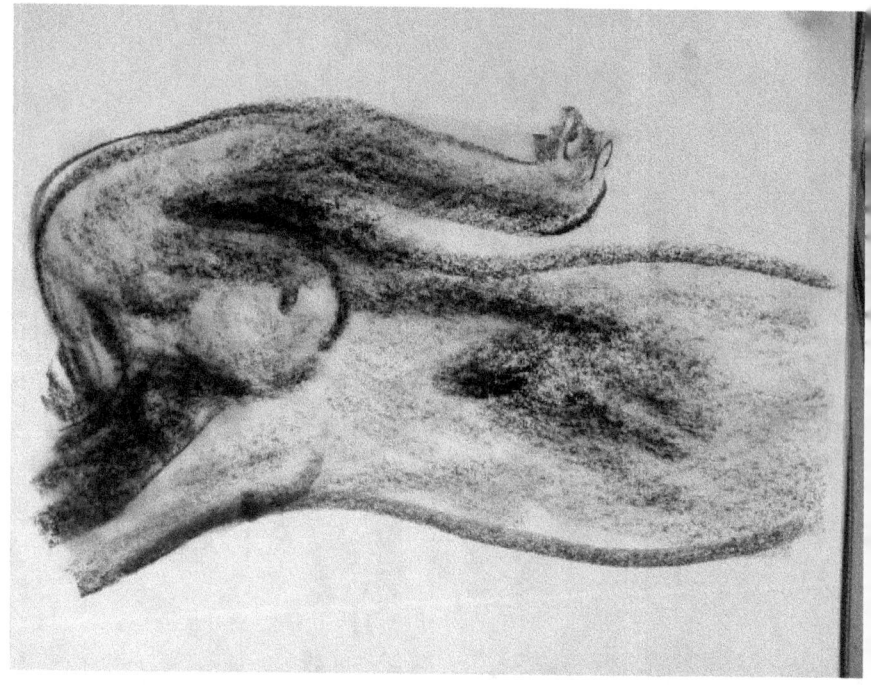

Fig 7:Woman leaning.

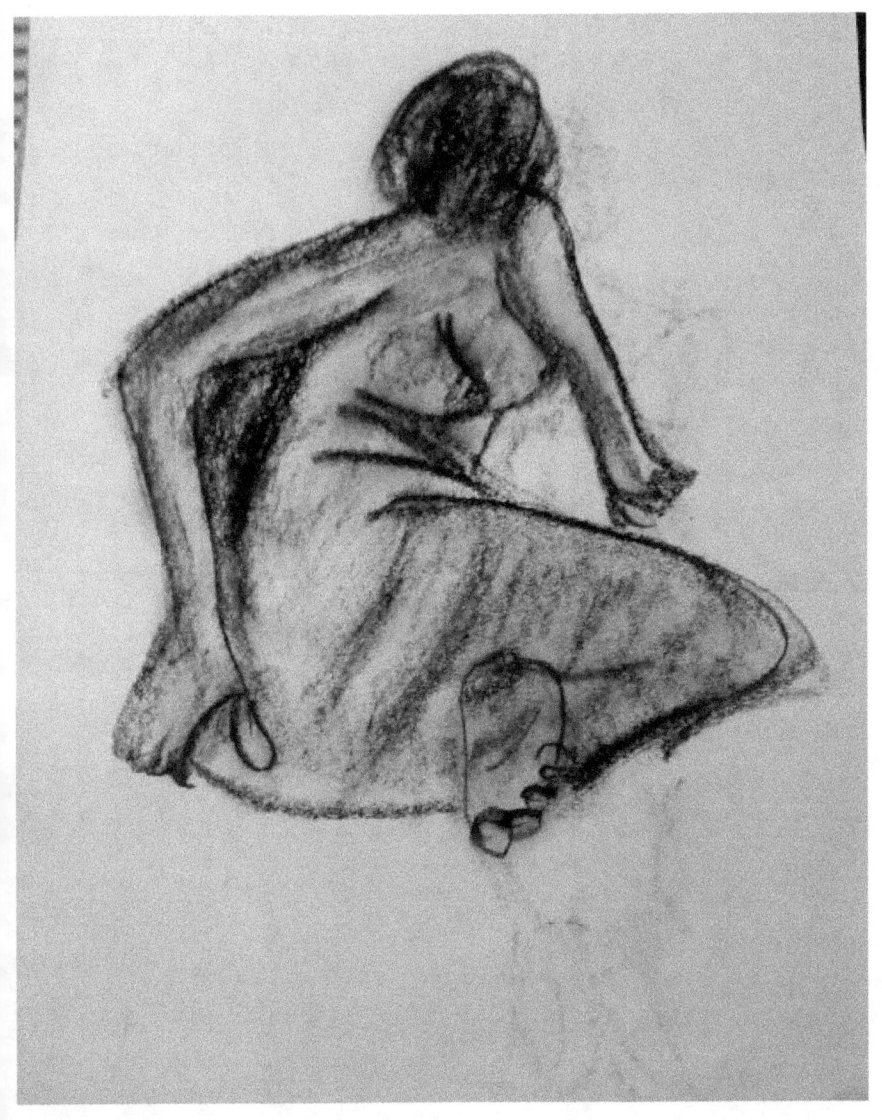

Fig 8:Old Man reclining

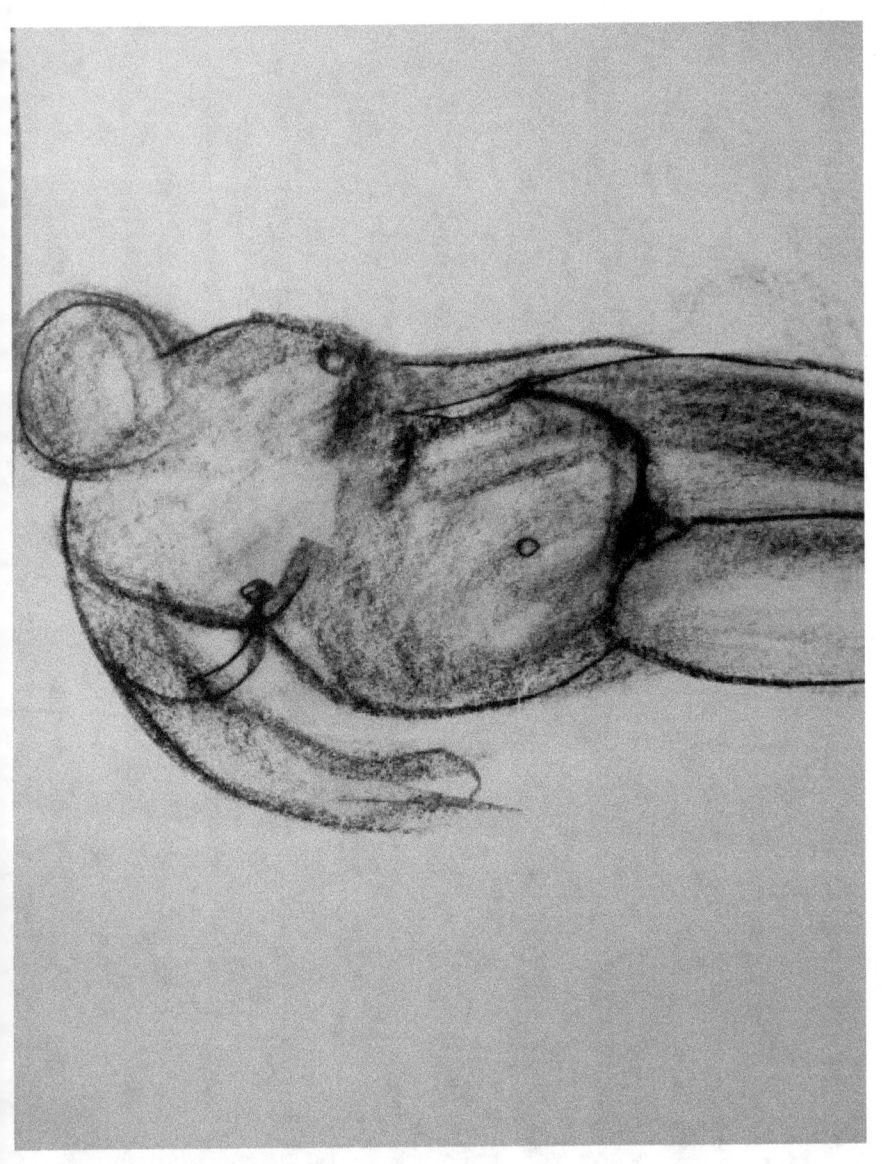

Fig 9:Back of man

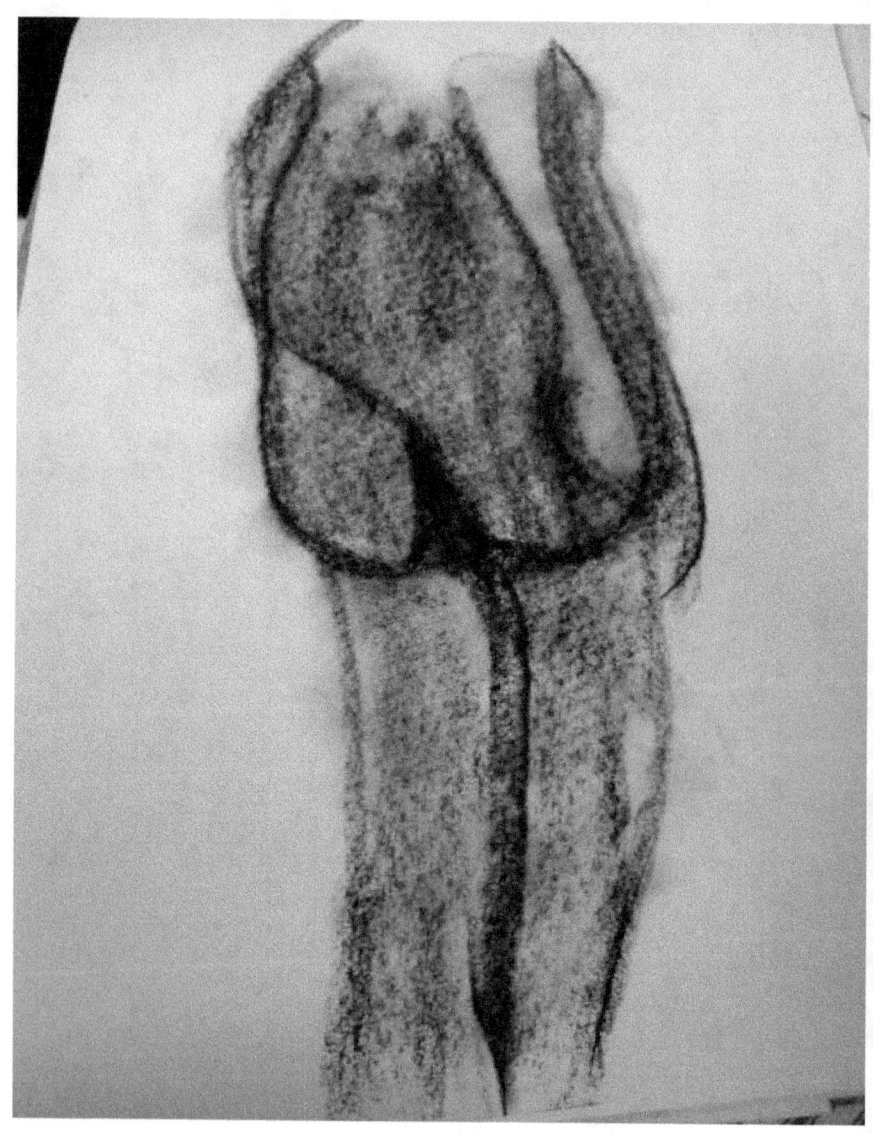

Fig 10:Front of woman

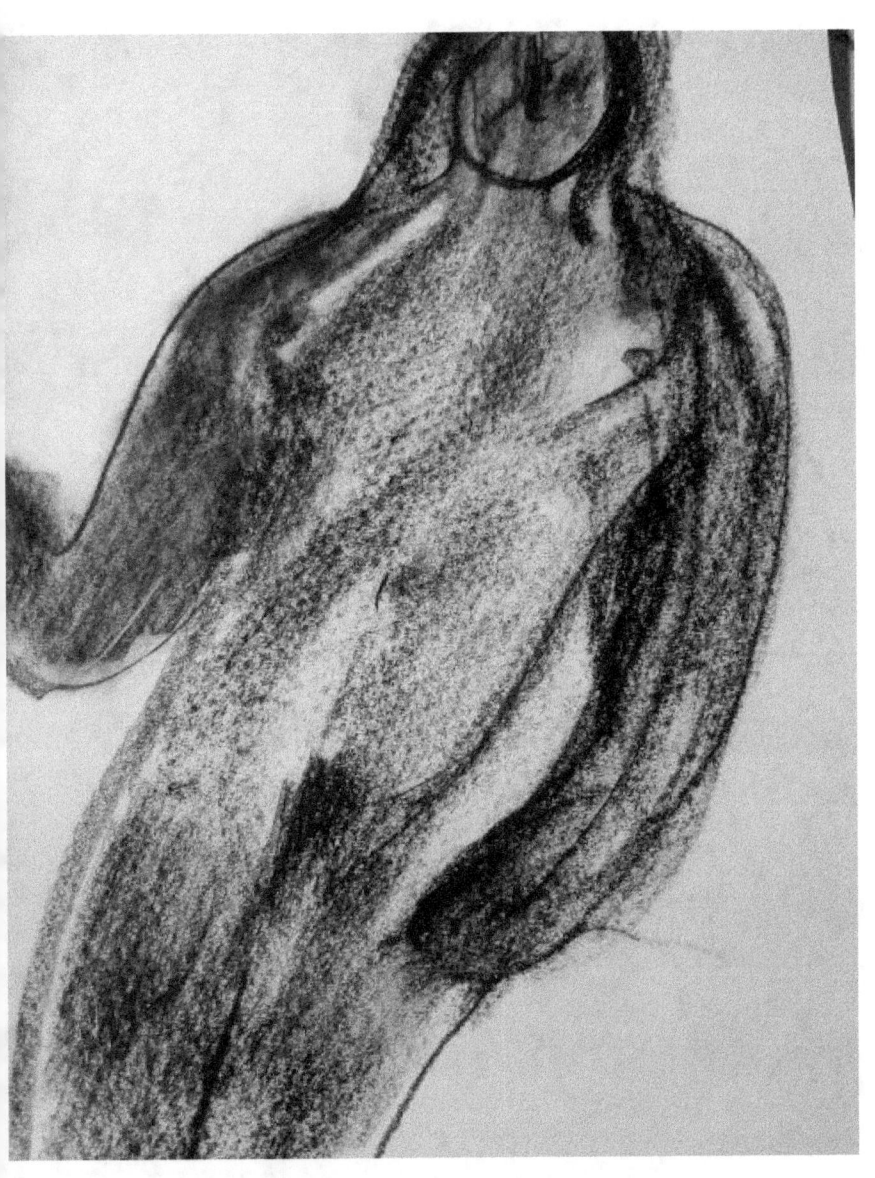

Fig 11: Girl on side

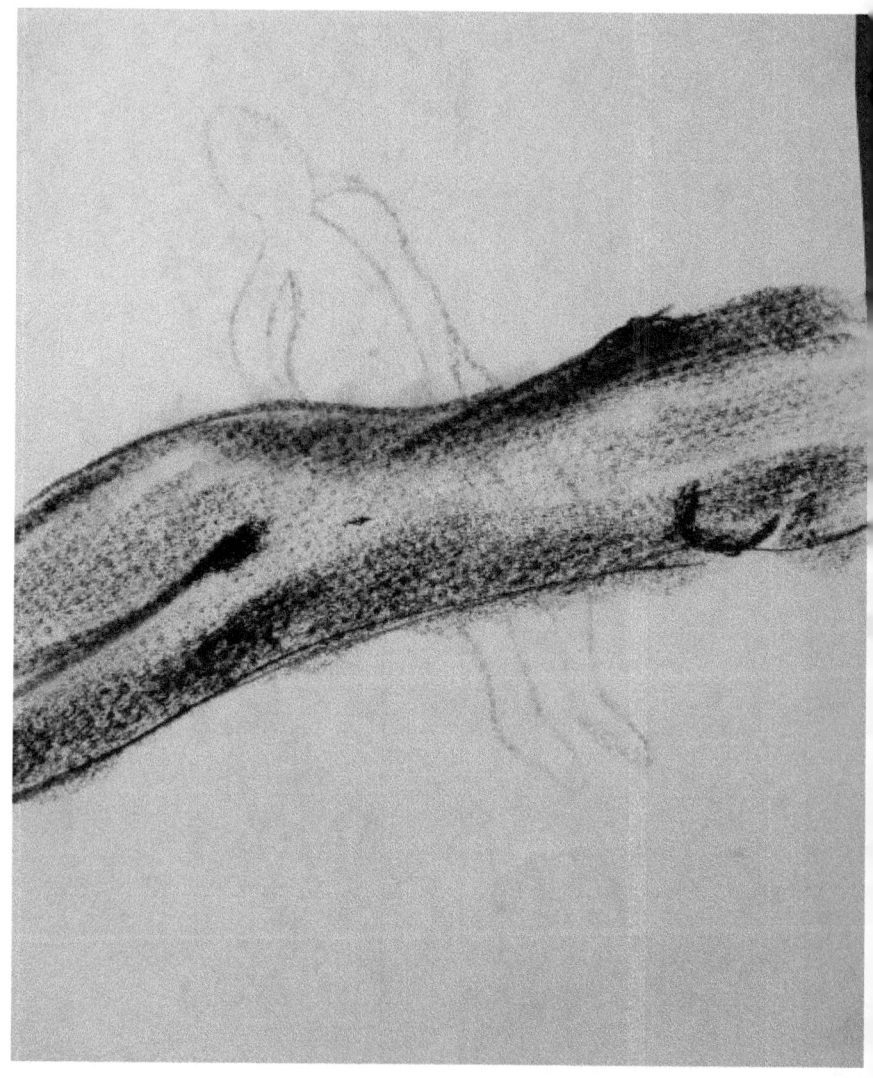

Fig 12:Girl sitting.

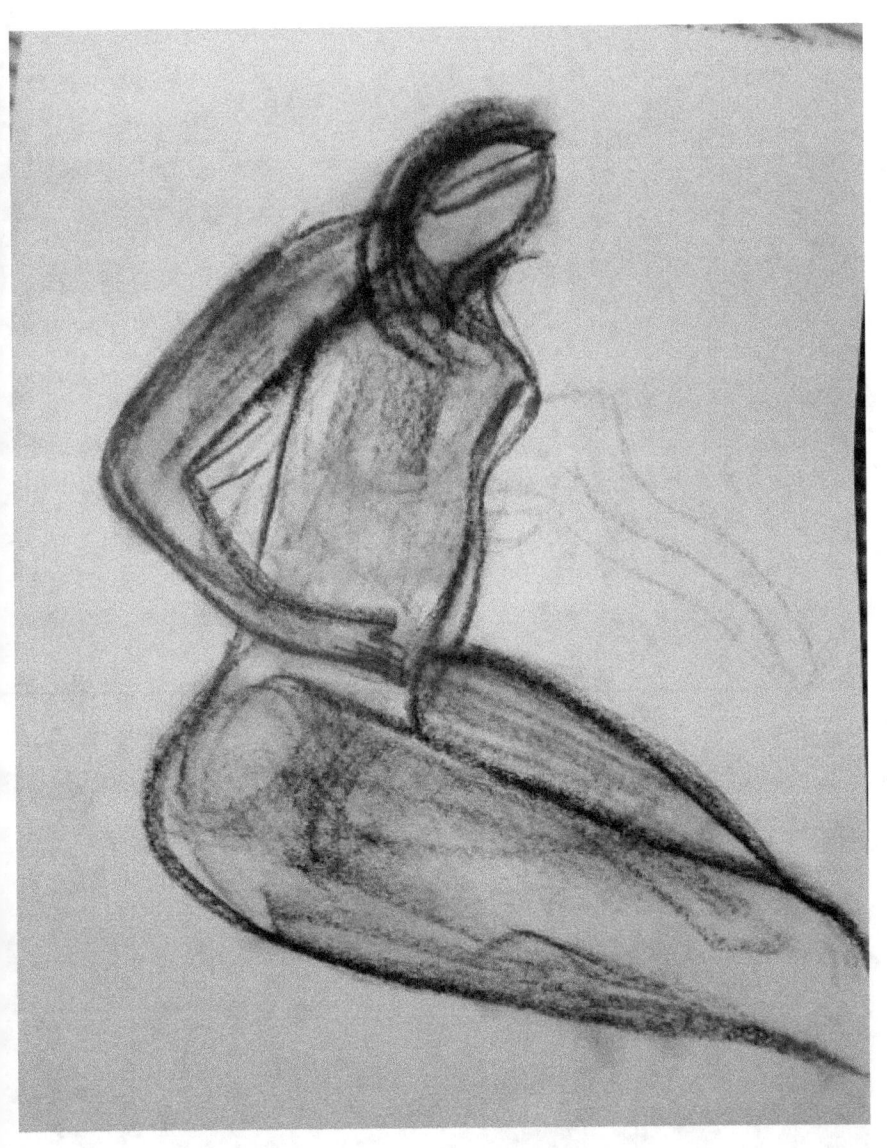

Fig 13: Girl at ease.

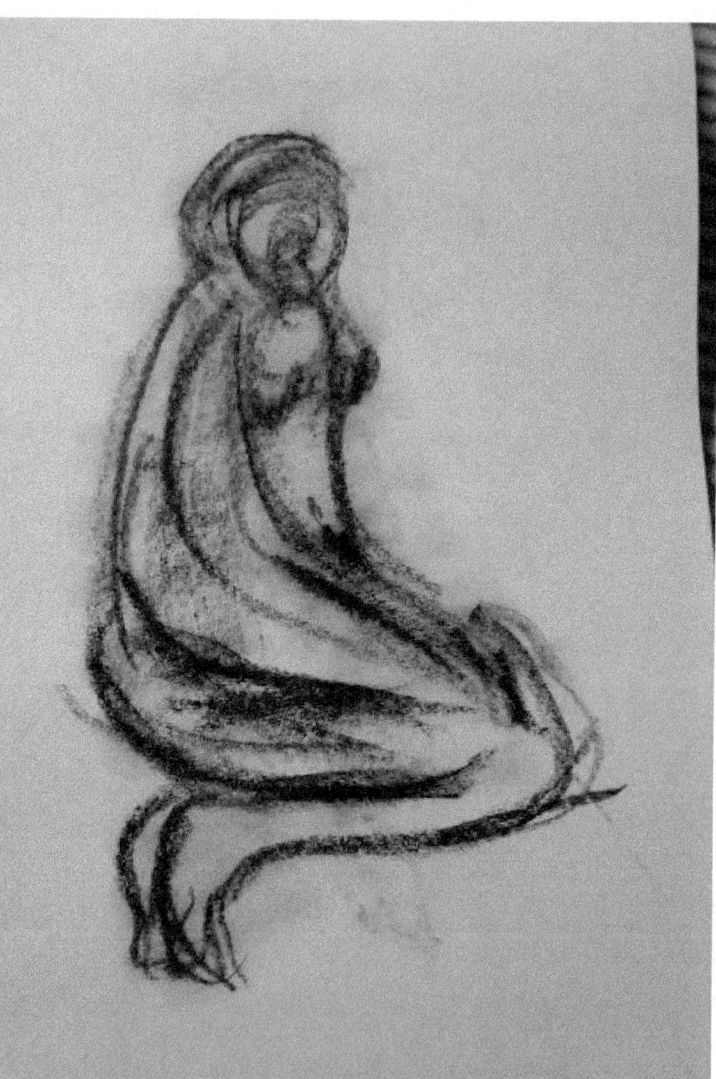

Fig 14:Girl leaning and sitting

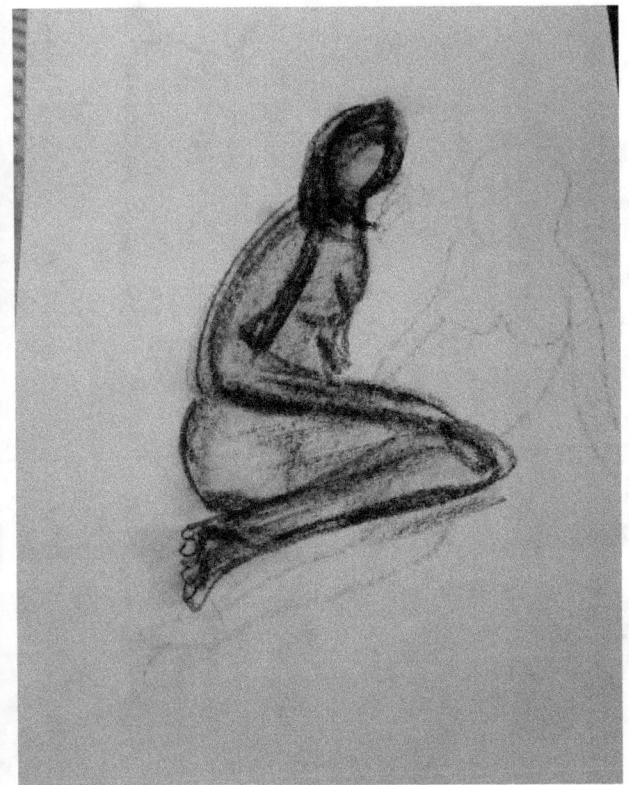

Fig 15:Woman with coat

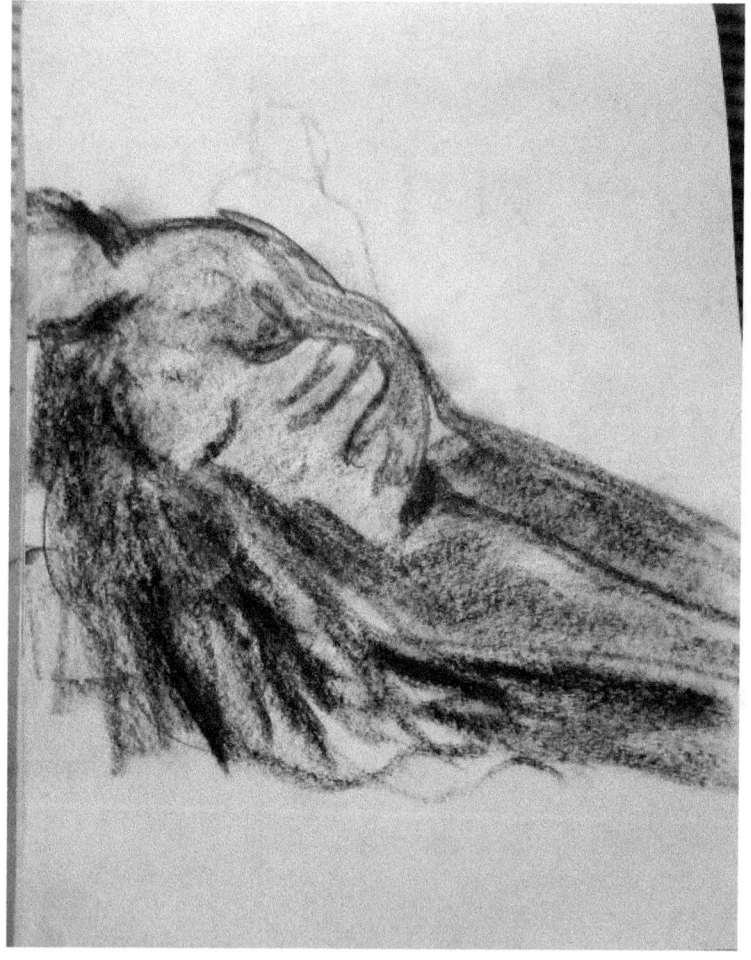

Fig 16: Woman with legs up

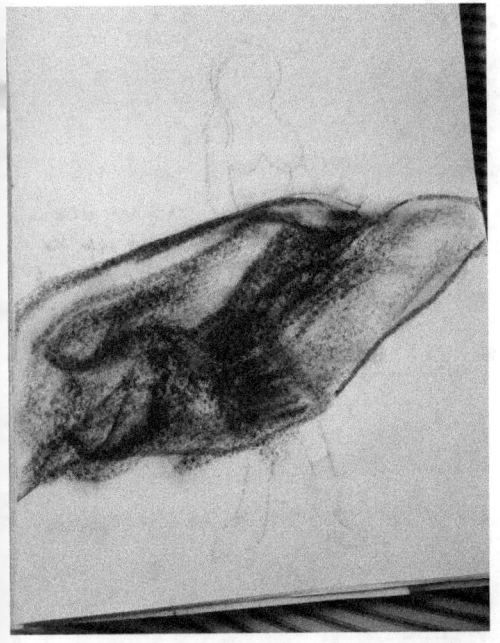

Fig 17: Woman's feet

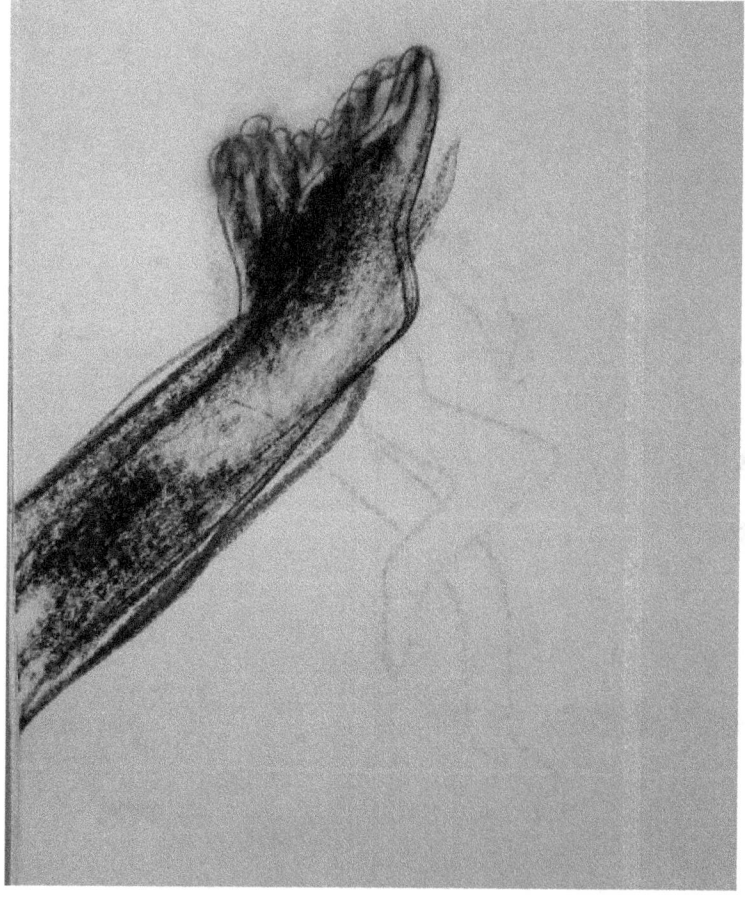

Fig 18: Woman lying down.

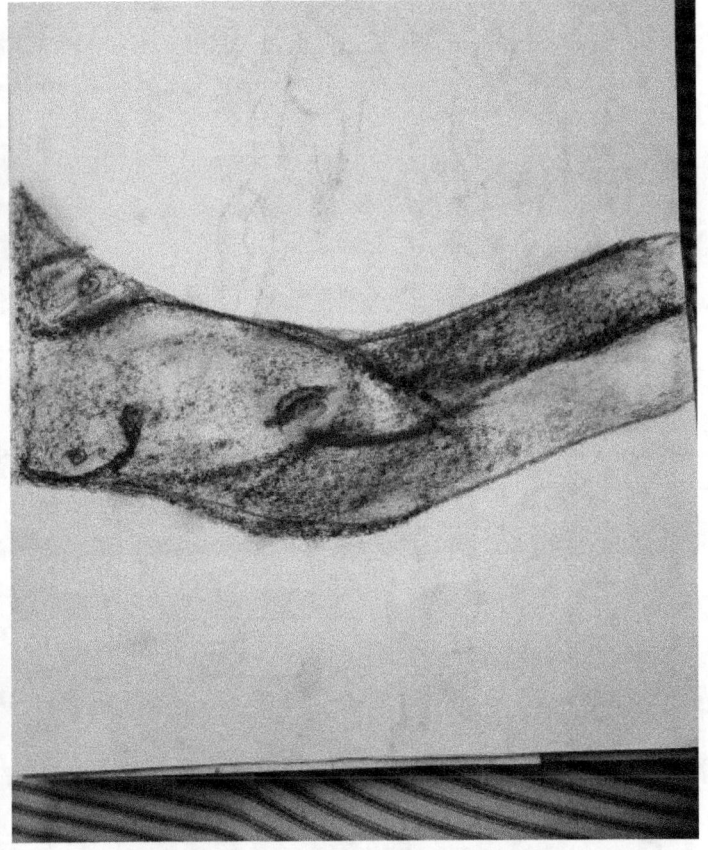

Fig 19:Sketch of nudes

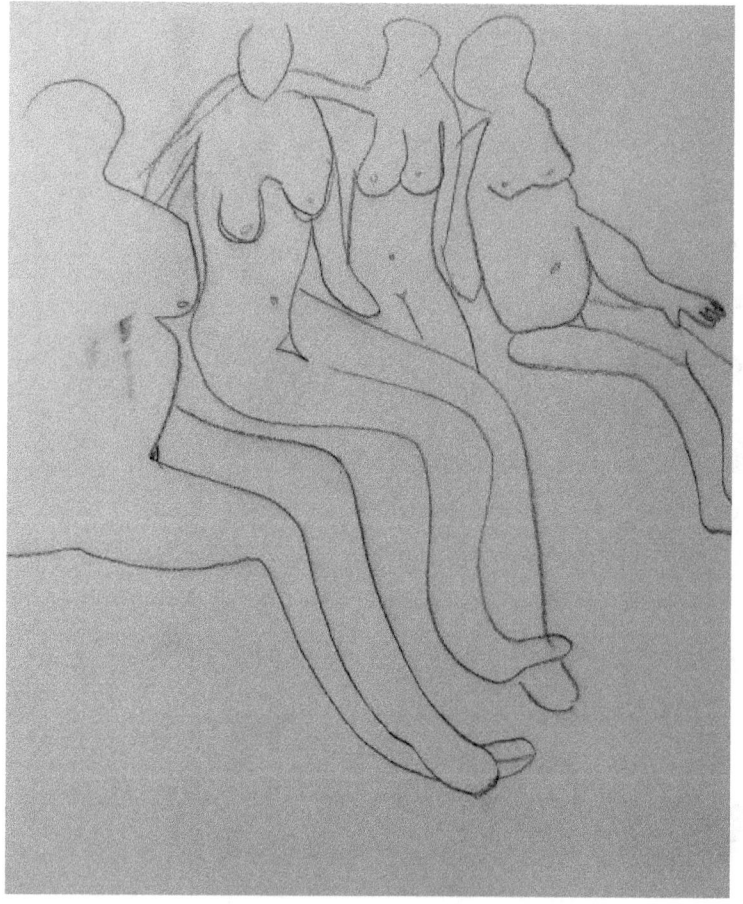

Fig 20: Singleline Female body

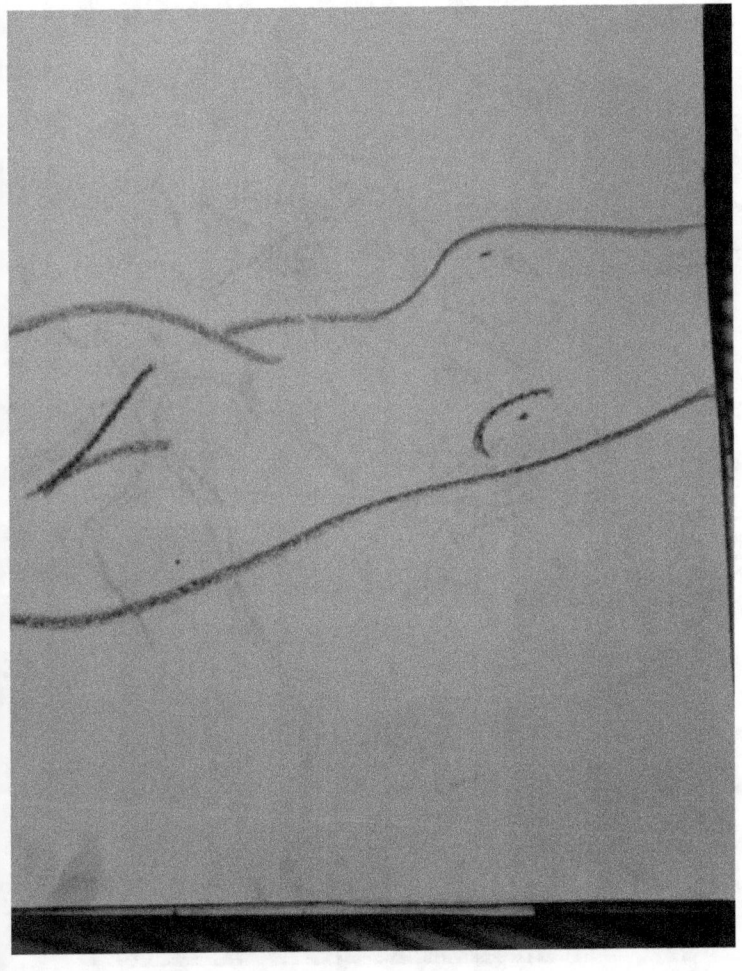

Fig 21: Comic sketch of woman.

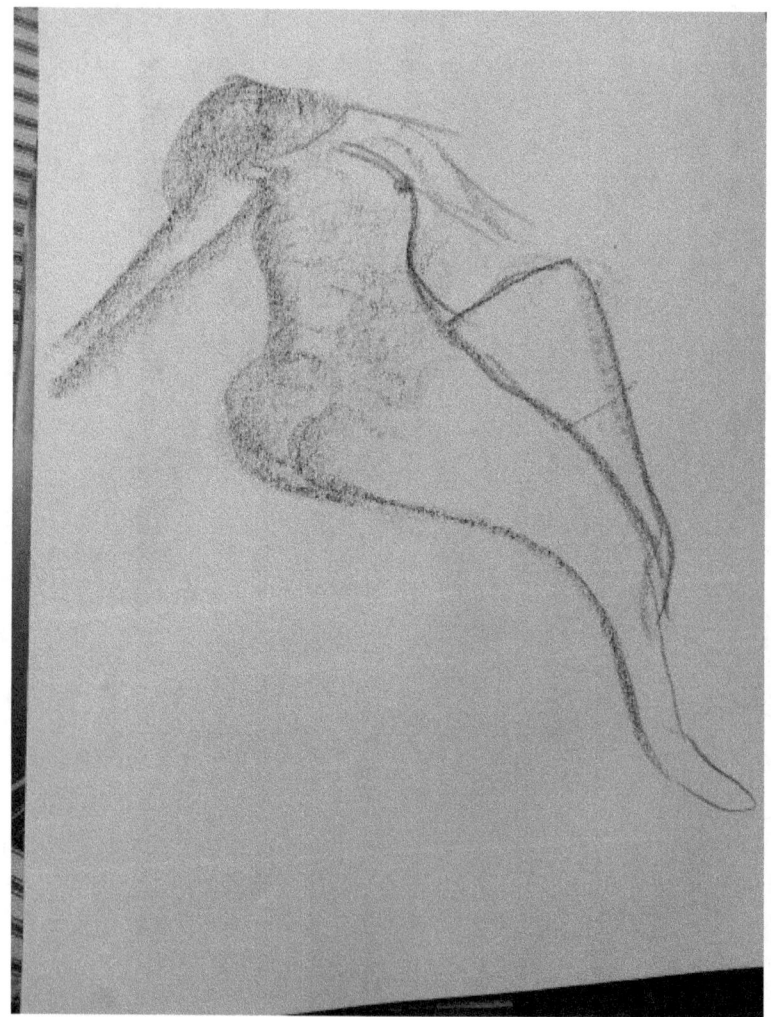

Fig 22:Woman sitting with crossed legs

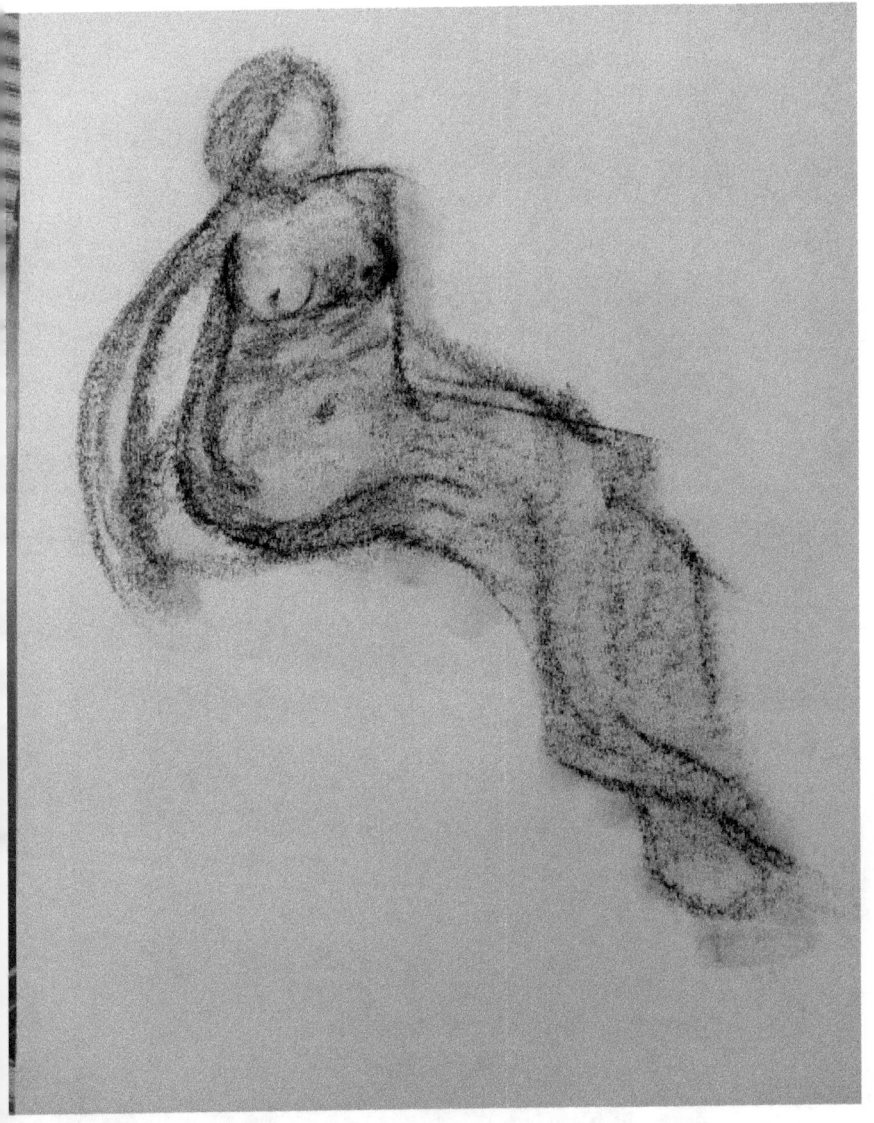

Fig 23: Two girls.

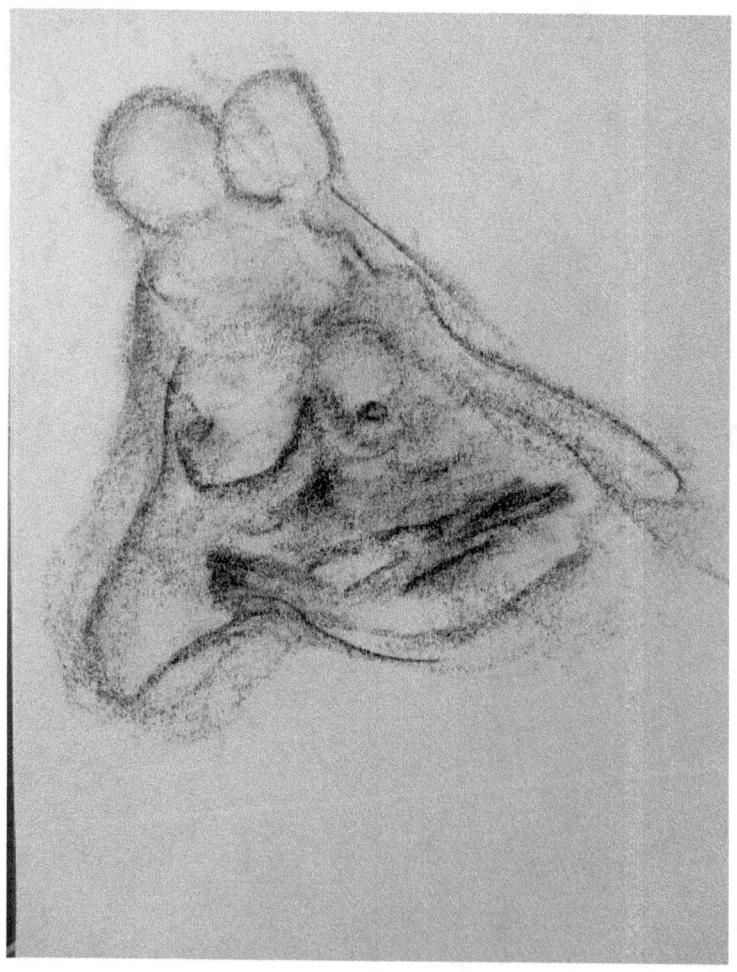

Fig 24: Woman with leg crossed.

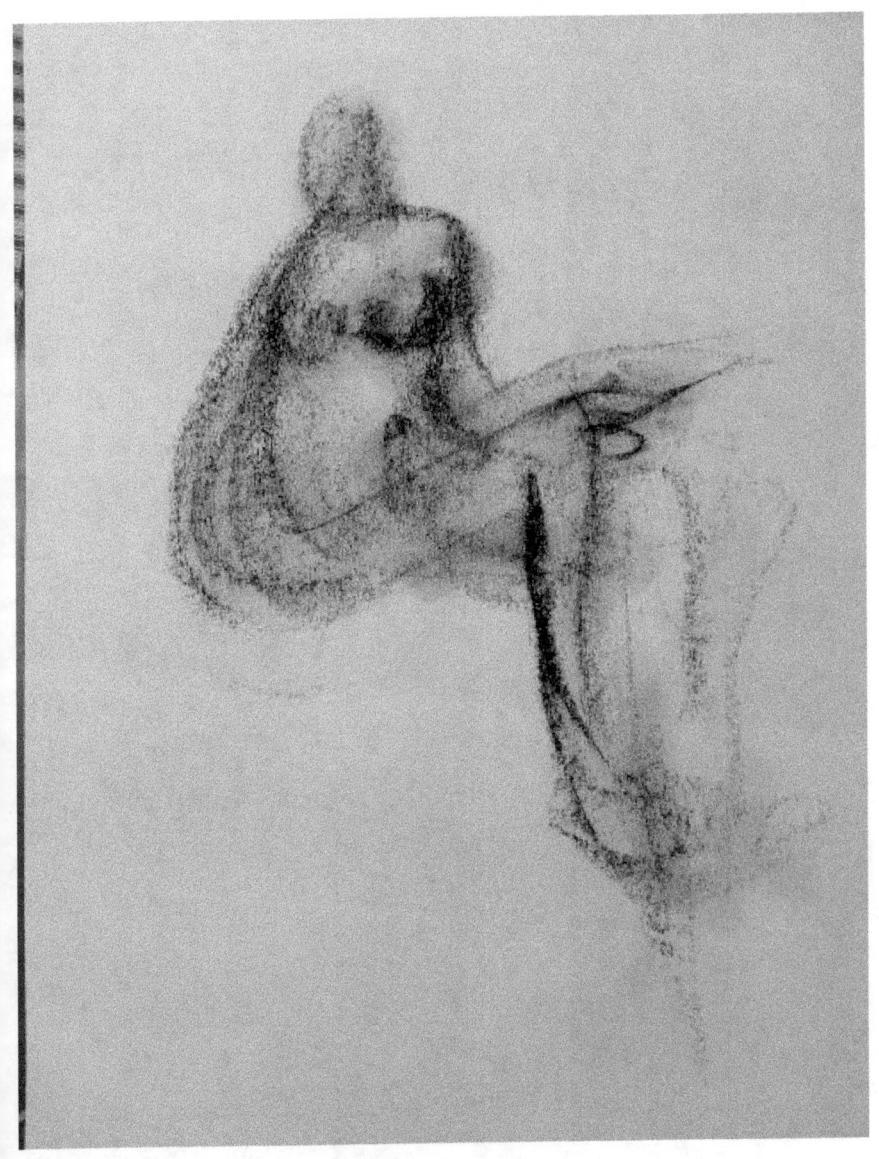

Fig 25: Fat old man.

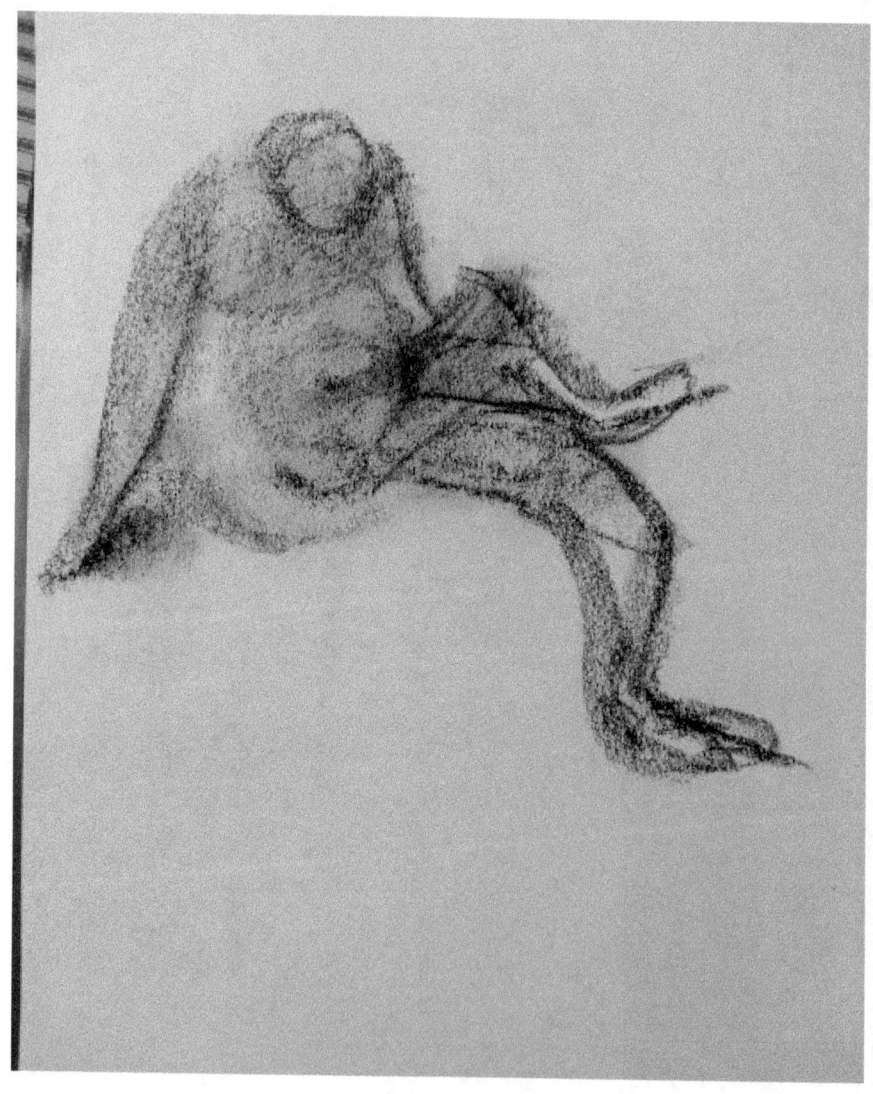

Fig 26: Woman with long legs.

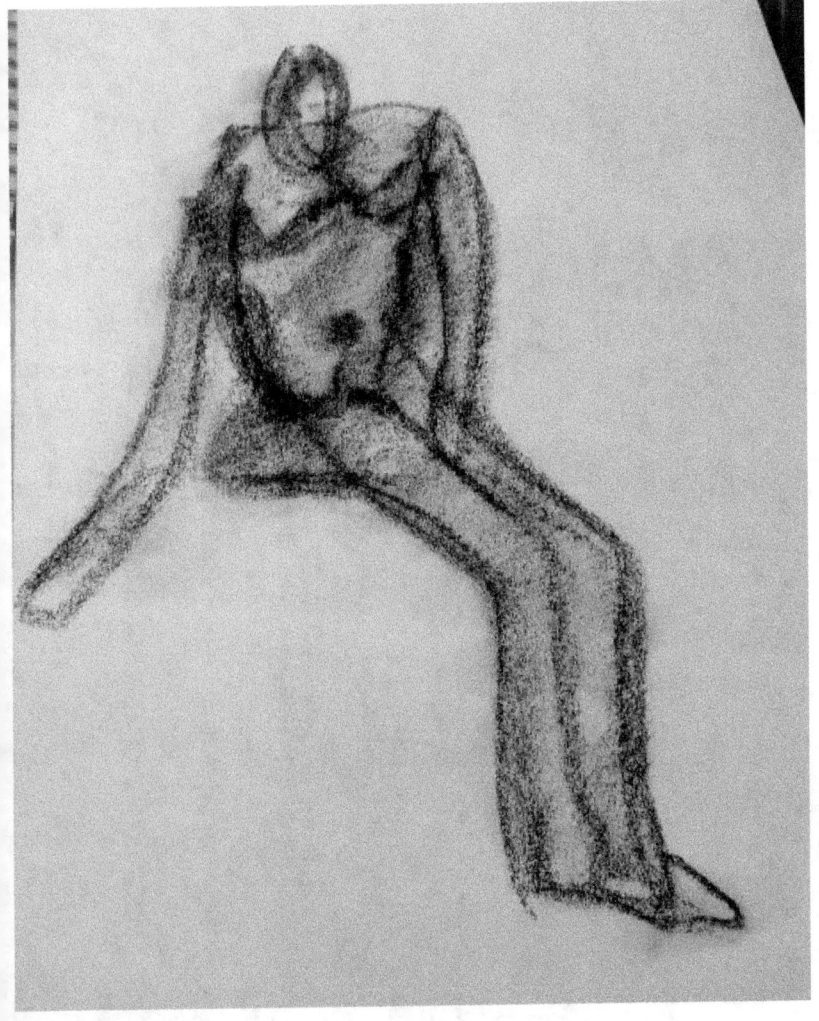

Fig 27:Man with leg crossed towards.

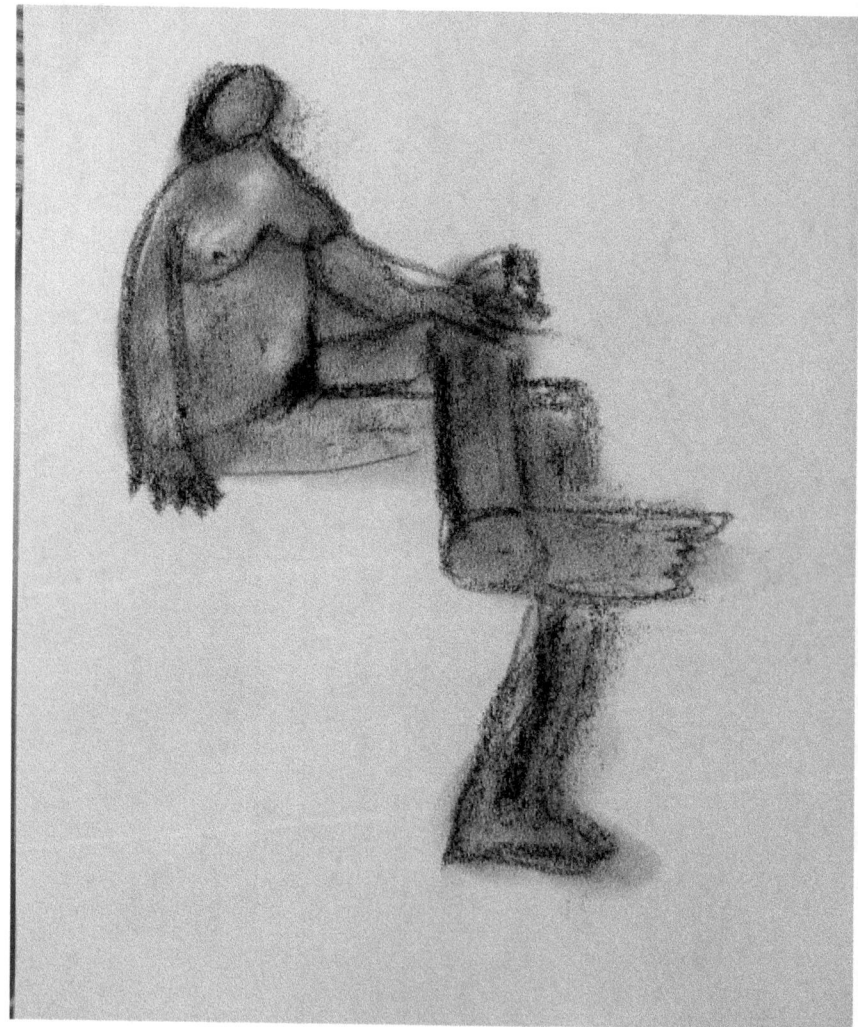

Fig 28: Front of woman

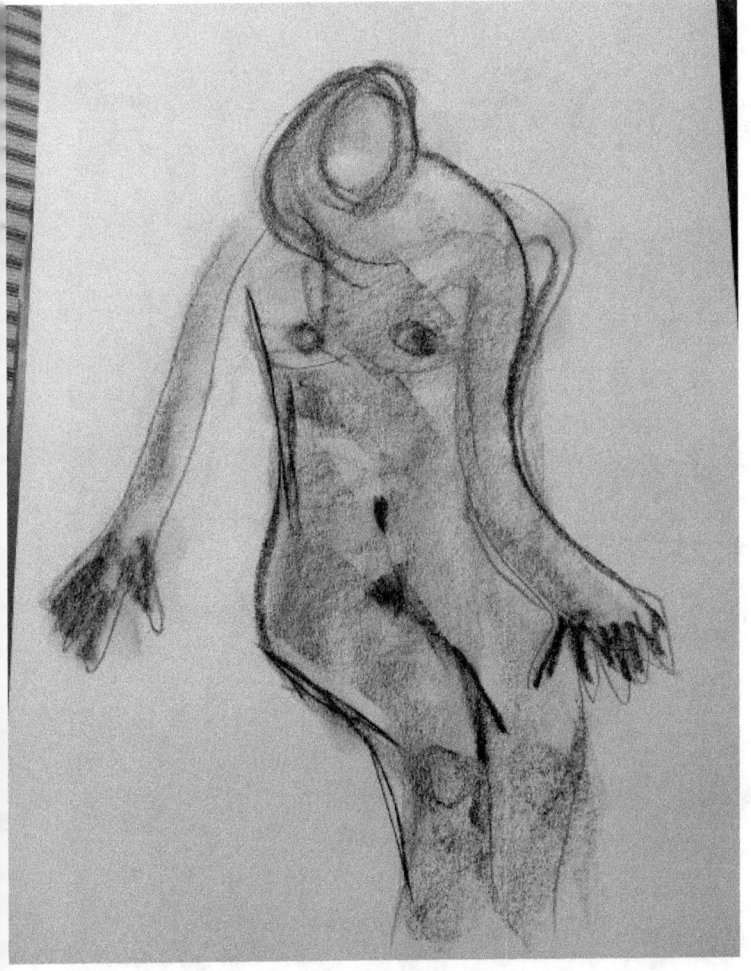

Fig 29: Young girl

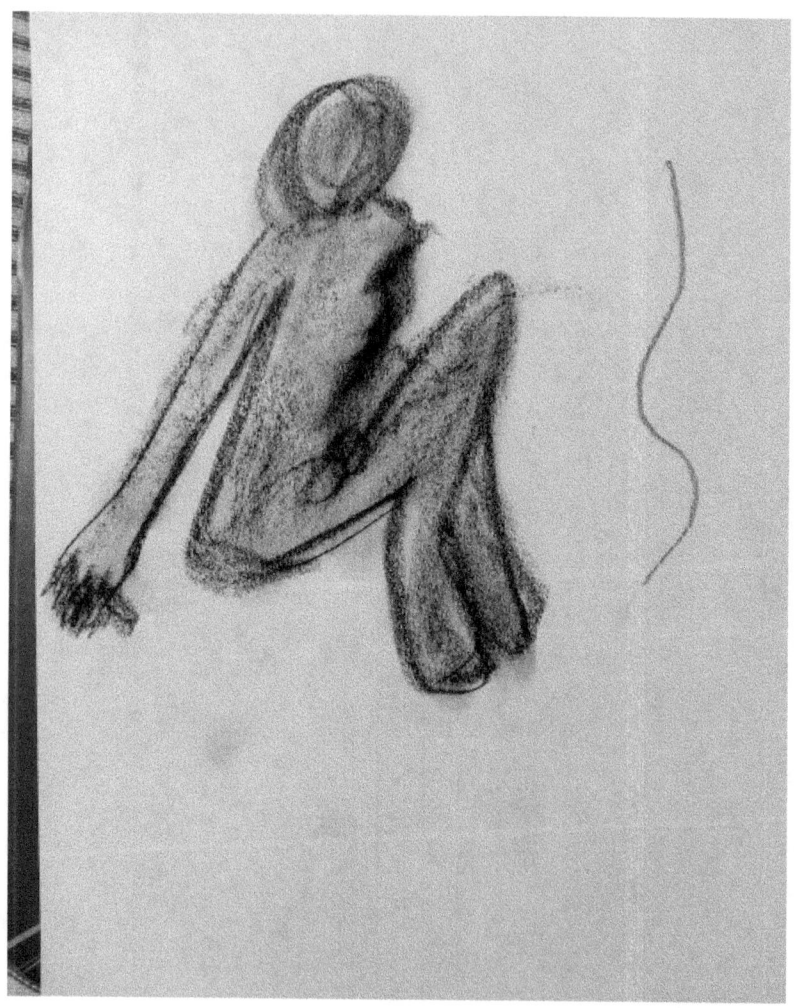

Fig 30: Woman's legs.

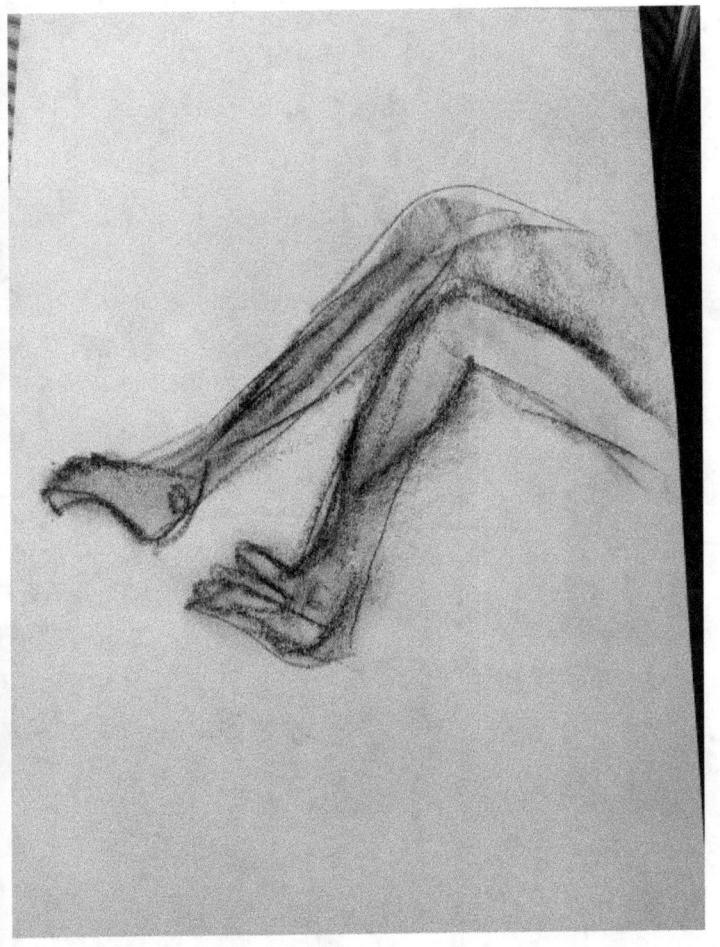

Fig 31: Young girl in shower

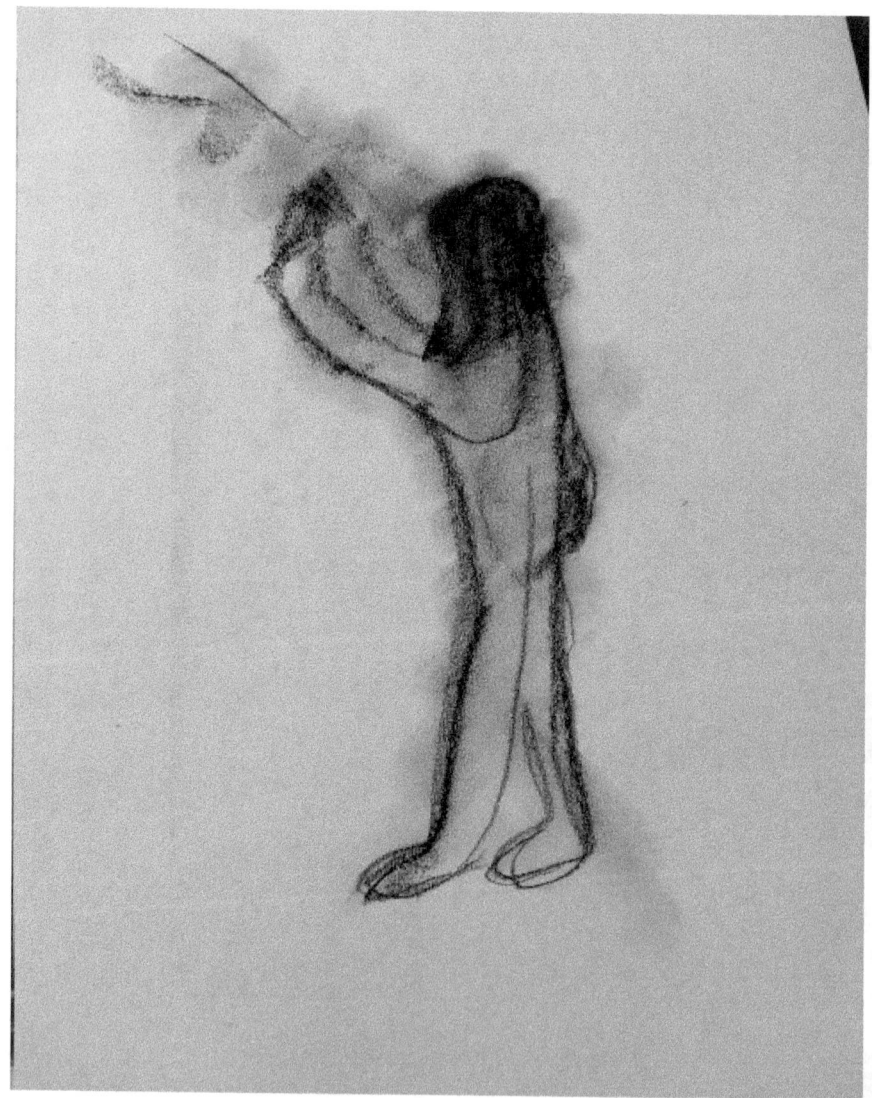

Fig 32: Girl on side with back toward.

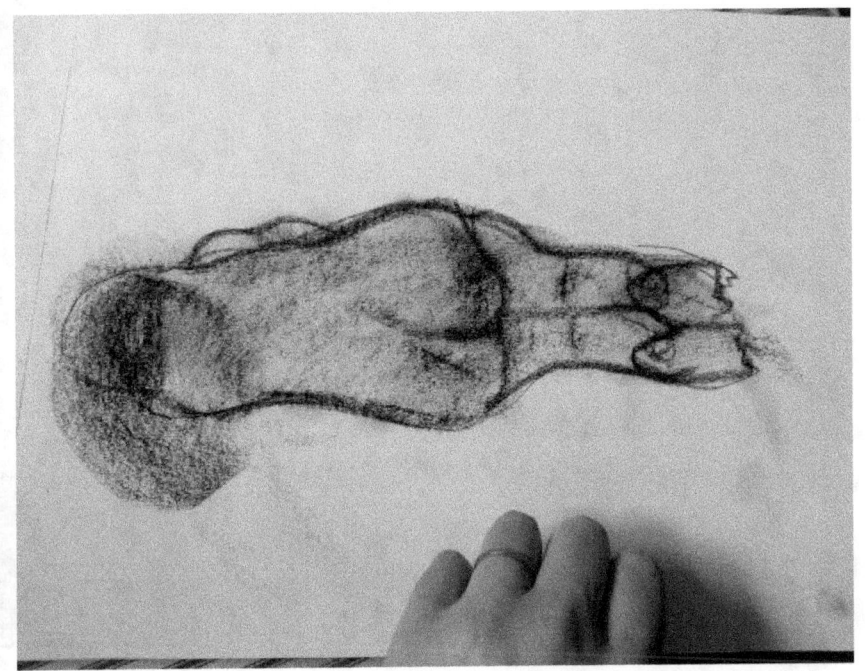

Fig 33: Woman on bed.

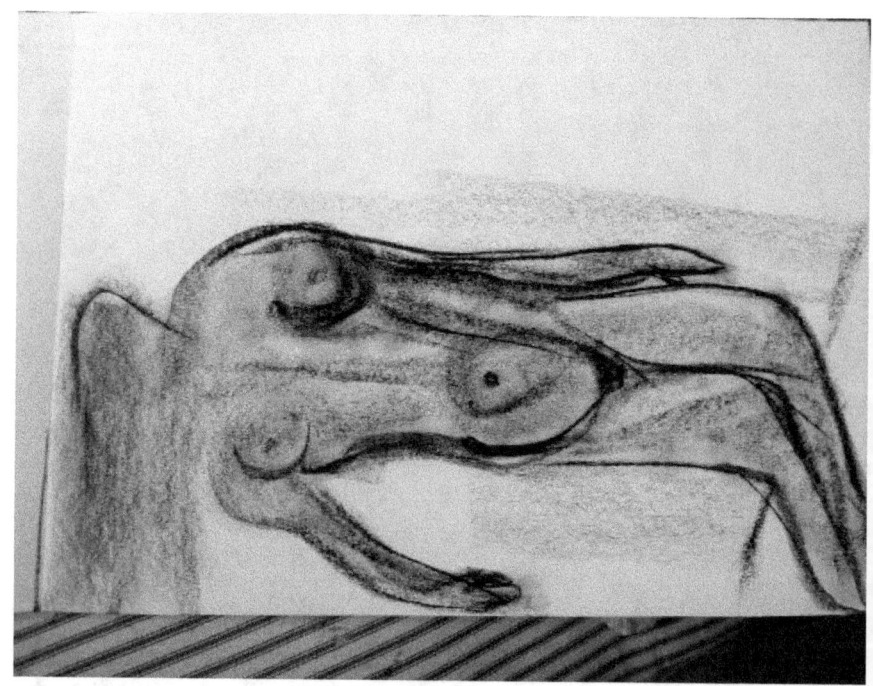

Fig 34: Woman by computer.

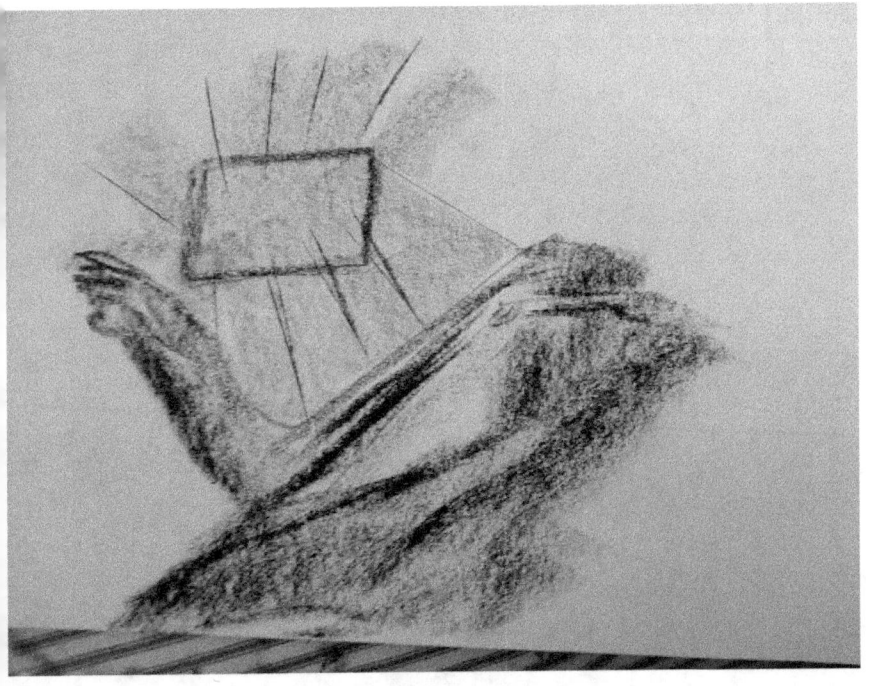

Fig 35: Woman tempting herself.

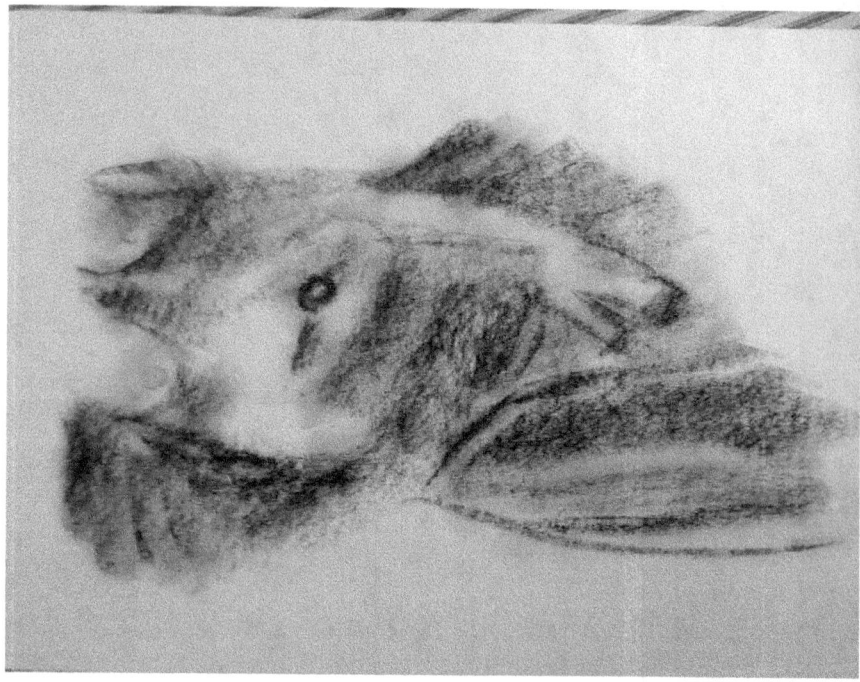

Fig 36: Woman on side reclining.

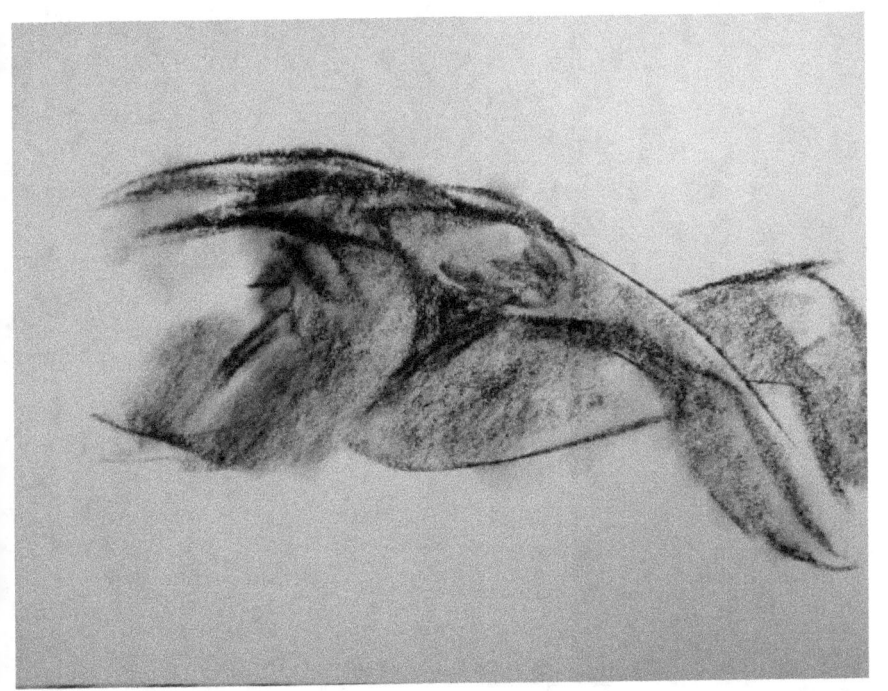

Fig 37: Woman's breast

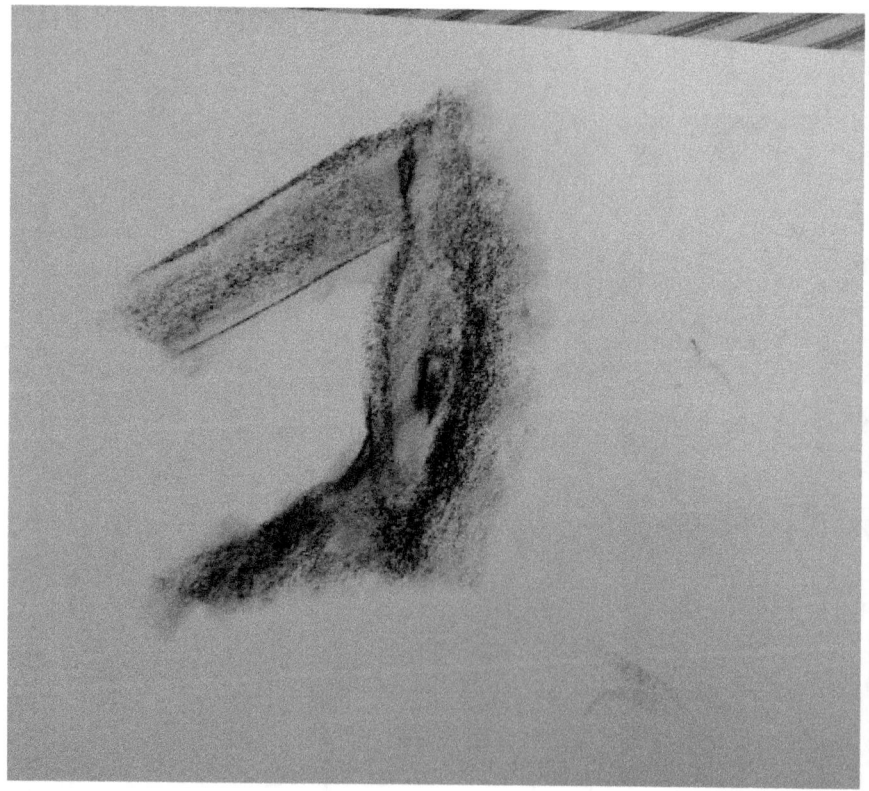

Fig 38: Woman's front

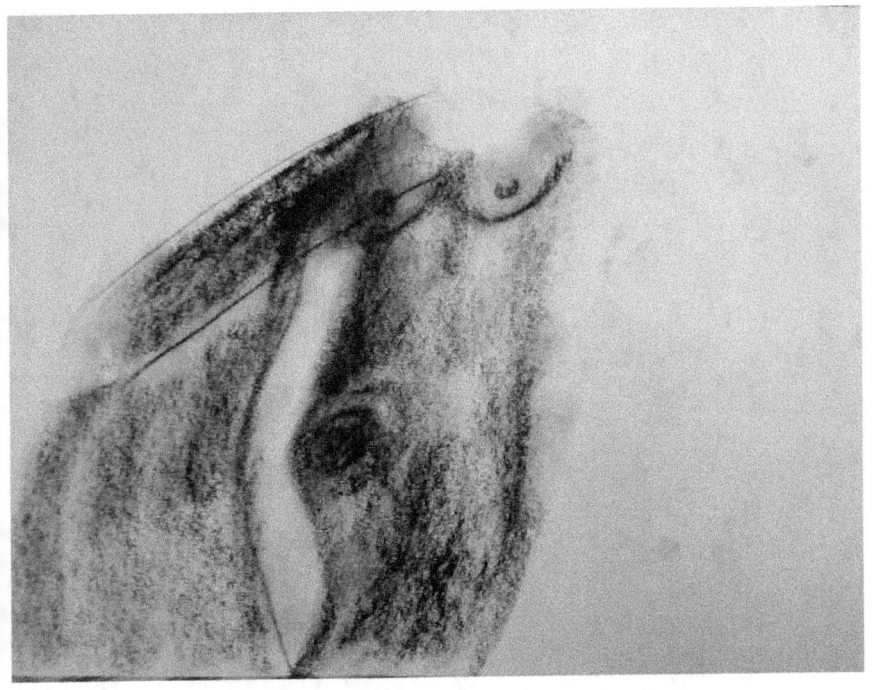

Fig 39 Woman's posterior

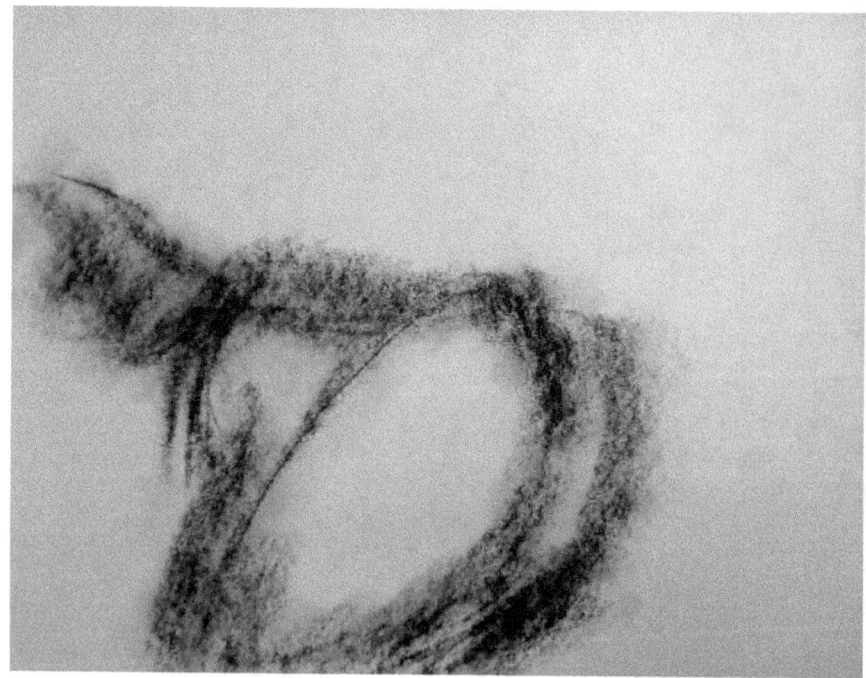

Fig 40:Woman in temptation

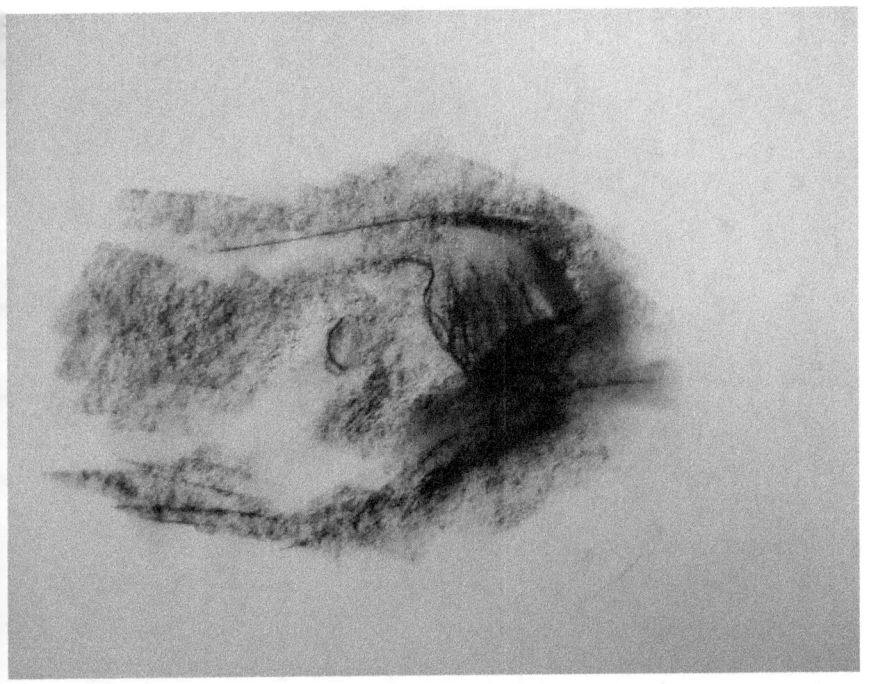

Fig 41: Girl in lotus position

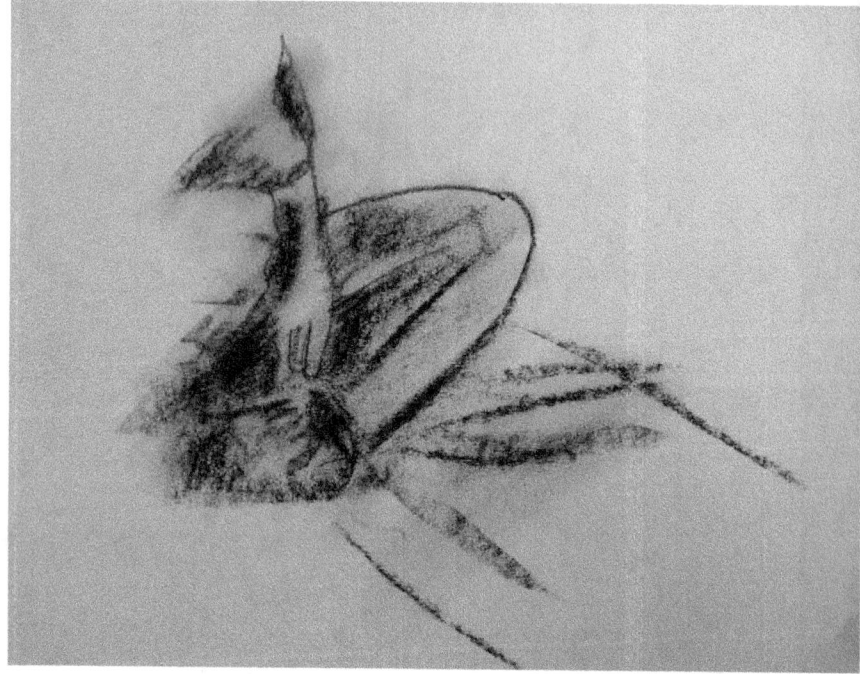

Fig 42:. Man's feet.

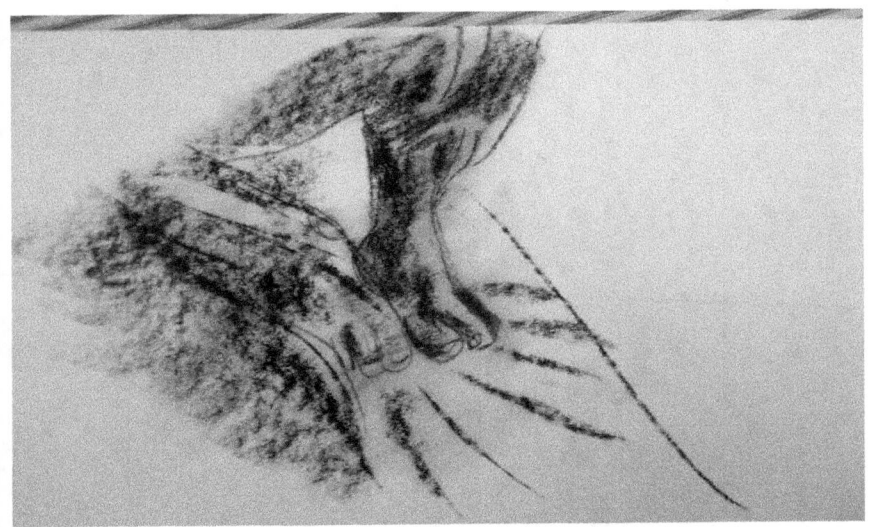